The Cowgirl's Guide to Love

She remains our foremost genuine American heroine adored internationally. She is part of our heritage and every generation, from the West or not, has a right to claim her.

— Joyce Gibson Roach, *The Cowgirl*

The Cowgirl's Guide to Love

Ellen "Lil" Patrick

BARNES
&NOBLE
BOOKS
NEW YORK

Published by MJF Books
Fine Communications
322 Eighth Avenue
New York, NY 10001

The Cowgirl's Guide to Love
LC Control Number 03-115445
ISBN 1-56731-661-1

Manufactured in the United States of America on acid-free paper ∞

MJF Books and the MJF colophon are trademarks of Fine Creative
Media, Inc.

QM   10 9   8   7   6   5   4   3   2   1

★ Table of Contents ★

Introduction

✶

Surely we are all at least dimly aware that harnessing the right man is not unlike catching an uncooperative horse. We of the more intuitive gender often must use our intelligent instincts and pretend to be terribly interested in something unrelated to the subject at hand, in order to arouse the curiosity of our prey. In fact, if you're like most cowgirls (trust me, you are), you probably *are* actually interested in just about anything other than this tedious business of bottle feeding some guy's bucking bronc of an ego. But there's more to it than that.

For generations, Cowgirls have conducted themselves by a Code that allows us to select and train the horse who is perfect for us, and to pursue a mutually rewarding, loving, and reciprocal relationship with that horse, often for the rest of our respective lives. Few things compare with the thrill of riding the trail on a sparkling summer morning, on the back of a horse you communicate with so well you only have to think a thought before your horse thinks it, too. You move as one being, yet you enjoy the world around you doubly for it, because of the absolute balanced perfection of your union.

I know it sounds corny. But it's true that the same analogy applies to you and your man – pro-

vided you apply what you know about being a
Cowgirl to what you know about being a woman.
And make no mistake: We are all Cowgirls at heart
(more about that in the next chapter).

The Cowgirl's Guide to Love represents the
bunkhouse low-down for the woman who is serious
about taming and training the male beast. I can't
lay claim to having invented this stuff. It has been
gleaned from late nights with other female wran-
glers around the campfire and out on the trail, during early mornings spent shoveling eggs and grits
onto plates and you-know-what out of stalls. I'd
like to think that this book is the first time this
body of ageless folk wisdom has been written
down. But I'd lay odds that somebody's Aunt Freda
or Sister Sal wrote it all before, in their letters of
advice to any number of young Cowgirls at any
number of times or places along the line.

Anyway, I'm just proud to be able to do my part
in sharing with all y'all this straight shootin' talk
that can help us Cowgirls do something about that
tendency we have toward being tough and smart on
the outside, and soft and stupid on the inside. The
folk wisdom contained herein can be used by any
woman, anywhere, on any man, anywhere. It was
invented by women in these United States, where
men are exceptionally childish and unruly, for the
purpose of creating and perpetuating a marginally
civilized society. You think men tamed the West?
Who do you think tamed the men?

Be careful when using the *Cowgirl's Guide*. It is powerful medicine. It works. If you use it on the wrong man, you'll be in trouble. You might get stuck with him. That's why it's important to understand, carefully select, and continue to understand your future romantic ride – a topic we'll explore in subsequent chapters.

But why, you might ask, if these guidelines are so well known and used by Cowgirls everywhere, must they be written down? The reason, for all of you who have been in a coma or a convent, or been co-opted by so-called feminism into behaving like common streetwalkers, is that – God forbid – our society is rapidly changing. The generations that are coming along, with their latchkey children, Gameboy addicts, and general self-worshipping trash, are in danger of losing their grip on the Code of the West (also known as the Code of Honor of these Great United States of America). This could spell the end of civilization as we know it. For, after all, if we lose our code of honor, we have lost our nation; perhaps even our world. And we will have certainly lost ourselves.

Thus, this little book is designed to keep intact our Cowgirl Code of living. I warn you, you might find it a little old-fashioned. Or maybe it's so old-fashioned that it's new-fashioned. It might even be radical. In fact, I heard it was banned in Atlanta. Whatever. Read it, use it, and you will remain forever happily in charge of that runny-nosed, moth-

er-conflicted, big-talking, insecure but adorable
John Wayne in your life.

CHAPTER ONE

Discovering Your
Inner Cowgirl

*I want to seize any pleasure that comes my
way because it might not come by again.
— Amelia Banks, 1901*

Kind reader, it pains me to even have to write this chapter. To think that there could be one woman out there who does not understand what is worth preserving forever in our leading archetypes is, well, a dismal prophecy for us all.

Make fun of her if you will. Pooh-pooh her passions if you must prove you are intellectually above it all. But never forget that Annie Oakley always got every single thing she ever wanted. She hit the bull's-eye every time, she beat every man and woman she ever went up against shooting stuff out of the air, she did it all over again from a galloping horse, and she had one of the happiest marriages in history. You might argue that she was a sellout, a comedic commercialization, even some kind of weirdo. God forbid you might say she was not actually a real Cowgirl.

It's true, our Annie was just a country girl from Ohio who accidentally discovered, using her daddy's rifle, a genius for a target. Shot a walnut straight out of a tree on her first try – when she was only seven years old. Did she ever work the range on a horse like a "real" Cowgirl? No. Did she know who she was and what she wanted, and pursued her dream in spite of all odds? You better believe it. In 1867, that was no mean feat for a little girl interested in shooting. If she can do it, you can do it, sister.

Don't tell me you don't have a vision for your life, hopes and dreams, ideas of love and happiness that you've often felt discouraged from achieving. Whenever that happens, just think about Annie Oakley and remember your own Inner Cowgirl. She's that part of you who hangs on and never gives up, no matter what. She's the you who longs to be happy and free and productive, loved and cherished and respected. She's the you who will make it through the toughest trail rides and beat out the fiercest competitors in this rodeo of life. Nuture her. Take care of her. And she will take care of you.

For example: when the man of your dreams comes along, it's your Inner Cowgirl who will help you recognize him and strategize appropriately for a lifetime of bliss. When the wrong man treats you like previously digested jimsonweed, it's your Inner Cowgirl who will pull you up out of the muck and help you regain your perspective. When you worry that you're not pretty enough, young enough, skinny enough, smart enough, or brave enough, it's your Inner Cowgirl who will yank you by your pigtail and slap you around, and make you laugh so hard you forget your foolishness. If you're sad, your Inner Cowgirl will cheer you up. If you need a friend, she is always there. And when you just don't think you can make it through another day, reach out your hand. There's your Inner Cowgirl, ready to pull you through.

If you've already got the horse-smarts to have all of the above figured out, then stop reading right

now and put down this book. You don't need it!
You need to go shopping or something. Lay back
on your pillow, congratulate yourself, and open a
box of bonbons. Or start writing your life story. But
if, like most of us, you range somewhere between
clueless and having things partially figured out,
read on. Join hands with your Inner Cowgirl! Even
better, join hands with your girlfriends and *their*
Inner Cowgirls! (Cowgirls are always there for each
other.) It's easy. Just remember the basic elements
of the Cowgirl Code and incorporate them, in your
own way, into your own life.

The Cowgirl Code

★ Always know very specifically what you want.

★ Never doubt that you can have exactly what you
want.

★ Never doubt that you are the most tantalizing girl
at the rodeo.

★ Remember that men aren't everything. They're
mainly someone to dance with.

★ Never let anyone tell you that you need to lose
weight, color your hair, get a face lift, lose your
accent, or change anything else about yourself that
you don't want to.

★ Take time every morning to prepare your mind,
body, and spirit for the day.

★ Never love a man you don't like.

★ Stay busy. The West wasn't won by women who laid around feeling sorry for themselves.

★ Be polite at all times – even while drawing your gun.

★ Be honest and true. A Cowgirl's Word is sacred.

★ Know when to use your spurs, and when not to.

★ Remember, if you can't say, "Yeehaw" to life every day, you just aren't living.

CHAPTER TWO

Know Your Horse, Your Man (and Your Self)

I wonder how many times I'm gonna fall for the same kinda cowboy.
— Bell Floyd, 1900

Before you do that thing Cowgirls do so well —
that is, torture men with longing and desire — be
sure you have the appropriate prey in your sights.

We'll go into this in more detail in the next two
chapters. But basically, there are two elemental
types of American male (be he urban, suburban, or
range-roving cowboy): the mama-dependent, and
the mama-deprived. Of course, there are endless
variations on type, but most men fall into one category or the other. This is important information for
two reasons. First, you must identify your animal
by type so you will know how to strategize his
management. Second (and most important), you
must be clear about what kind of man is right for
you, so you don't accidentally end up with the
wrong one. This happens more often than any of us
would like; hence, the endless roster of divorces,
even on the rodeo circuit.

It can help to think of your ideal man, at least
initially, in the way you would think about your
ideal horse. I know, I know, it's entirely likely that
you have never set your butt on the back of a
horse. It's entirely likely you don't want to. It's even
likely that you've never even seen a live horse
unless it was pulling a carriage around Central
Park or holding up a mounted police officer. No
matter. Your actual experience with riding and
horsemanship is irrelevant right now. What I'm
talking about, really, is your personality and personal preferences. I'm using the analogy of horse

and rider because a Cowgirl's choice of horse is the absolute foremost outward expression of her most personal self.

As every riding gal will tell you, it's easy to let outward appearances lead you astray. You might fall in love with that glossy blond palomino, only to find that you can't bond with him because he's head shy. You might have your heart set on a gaited horse, only to end up with a Tennessee Walker whose legs are unsound. That glorious Appaloosa you've dreamed of making your next best friend may turn out to be a biter.

So what do you want? A cuddly type who will practically beg you to nap with him in his stall? An older horse who won't bolt at top speed for the nearest alfalfa field? Or one of those who will run all day with the wind in his mane? Maybe you are the caretaking type who will blossom with a needy horse who requires lots of patience and retraining? A down-to-earth gal in search of an all-round cow pony? A rodeo princess dreaming of her ideal show-stopping stud?

You've got to start by knowing yourself. That way, when the wrong horse/guy turns your head, you have a prayer of controlling your reactions so you don't make a mistake and get hurt. Since the next two chapters will talk about your man, let's talk about you now by looking at the Three Basic Types of Cowgirl.

Which category best describes you?

Are You a Calamity Jane?

(Always saving people, worrying about others, stepping in and saving the day)

- Do you enjoy taking care of people, the way Calamity selflessly nursed the smallpox-afflicted citizens of Deadwood?

- Would you be perfectly content if caring for a family were your sole occupation in life?

- Would you sacrifice your life for home and hearth?

- Is a job or career secondary or irrelevant to you?

- Do you like to cook – a lot?

- Do you tend to be a thoughtful advisor rather than the leader of the pack?

- Do you derive pleasure from supporting and enhancing the interests of others?

- Do your hobbies keep you in or revolve around the home?

- Do you spend time or have the urge to spend time in good works for the benefit of the community? Do you take in strays?

- Are you the type who gets a thrill out of showing unexpected kindness to strangers?

If you answered yes to seven or more of the questions above, you are the Calamity Jane type and will be happiest with the mama-dependent man.

Are You a Lady Godiva?

(Following your own path, even if it means riding naked on a horse to prove a point)

- Are you moody and sometimes considered by others to be "difficult?"

- Do you have a way of charming strangers with your whimsicality and ethereal nature?

- Do you feel confined when you are forced to spend too much time at home?

- Do you relish the idea of being out in the world, having lots of new experiences?

- Have you had lots of boyfriends, or have lots of men had crushes on you?

- Are you a dreamer at heart?

- Do you basically expect others to adapt themselves to your needs?

- Do you tend to be rather undisciplined?

- Are you lacking in domestic skills?

- Do you have an artistic or creative bent?

If you answered yes to seven or more of the questions above, you are a Lady Godiva type, and will be happiest with a slightly mama-dependent man, or a very toned-down version of the mama-deprived.

Are You an Annie Oakley?

(Rarely wavering from your mission in life, got your eyes on a higher goal)

- Have you worked your fingers to the bone in your single-minded determination to get ahead?

- Is your career all-important to you? Would you describe yourself as driven?

- Would you feel frustrated if you were to devote your entire life to family?

- Do you have little patience with the neediness of others?

- Are you highly focused and goal-oriented?

- Do you expect to be waited on from time to time?

- Do you have a very busy life with little time for dating?

- When you have a leisure moment, would you prefer to be home with a good book rather than out with a man you're not intensely interested in?

- Do you have little interest in what people think of you? Do you find yourself impatient with the niceties of society?

- Do you dislike making small talk?

If you answered yes to seven or more of the preceding questions, you are an Annie Oakley and will be happiest with the mama-deprived man.

If you find you don't totally fit any one of the three categories above, don't worry. These are archetypes designed to get you thinking about what kind of man you need. If you're like most women, you will have a lot of Calamity Jane in you, because most of us are raised by our mamas to think we have to wait on a man hand and foot. But just because you were raised that way, don't think you have to be that way. Take a close look at yourself. Have you always rebelled against that sort of thing and hated the way men expect you to hold out a pan and catch their tobacco plug for them? You don't have to, child. On the other hand, if you truly enjoy taking care of someone lock, stock, and barrel – go for it.

The point is, know the kind of man you want before you go after him. According to the time-honored principles of the Cowgirl Code, of course. And no matter how pretty, charming, sugary-talk-ing, or heroic that next irresistible male might be, if he doesn't fit your needs, don't even try him on! If I could only get my girlfriends to remember this, we'd all be a lot better off.

Do you know the real story of Lady Godiva? She was an aristocrat who lived in England in the eleventh century. She and her husband, Leofric, Earl of Mercia, shared a deep religious faith and community spirit. Together, they bestowed funding on many worthy projects to improve their town.

Lady G. was an accomplished horsewoman, by the way. She also happened to nurse a fervent passion for the arts. In fact this sexy, gutsy, artsy, early Cowgirl was so convinced of the value of the arts that she told her husband he needed to lower taxes, so the townsfolk could afford to be artsy, too!

The Earl was a pretty big firebrand in his own right, and he told Godiva that if the arts were so important to her, she should do something to prove it. He challenged her to ride, in the nude, on her horse through town. Like a true Cowgirl, Lady G. was not one to back off a challenge. Quite the opposite. She called his bluff and did it. Impressed with her brass, hubby Earl cancelled taxes. What they did behind closed castle doors later that night is anyone's guess, but mine is that they got it on big time. What a pair. The moral of the story is that Lady G. had herself a man who matched her type of Cowgirl spirit. Just think how miserable she would have been with some stick in the mud, no matter how cute or rich he was.

CHAPTER THREE

The Mama Factor

Wanted: Cowboy— Nice looking,
affectionate, good-natured.
— Mary Jane, 1875

As we have mentioned in the previous chapter, cowboys (read: men) fall into two basic categories: the mama-dependent and the mama-deprived. I don't care how much they try to hide the fact with big-boy macho talk or new-age sensitivity, they are all the product of their mamas. I can't emphasize enough how important this is in choosing your ideal mate and strategizing his management and care: You MUST identify the nature of his mama-conflict.

There are two kinds of males because there are two kinds of mamas. First, you have the mama who lays her life down for her children. Your basic martyr, she lives for her children, especially her boys, and cooks and cleans for them even when they are forty years old. This kind of mama will wipe their boogers and pick up their underwear behind them until the day she dies.

What this type of mama creates is the classic mama-smothered male. A man who expects you to wait on him just like his mama did. A man who, with the proper training, can be a hearty provider and healthy romantic partner, but who will always be, to some degree, on the childish side.

This is no great sin. Very few of us, male or female, ever truly reach full maturity. And if you are a Calamity Jane type, who needs a man who needs lots of taking care of, this may be just the type of man for you.

But it is important that you recognize what kind of man you are dealing with under the surface, before you use your Cowgirl medicine full-strength on him. That way you won't find yourself stuck with the wrong kind of beast. (I don't think I have to tell you how hard a bad cowboy can be to get rid of, but more on that subject later.) Here's a handy checklist to use on the trail:

The Mama-Dependent Male

☞ Chews with his mouth open because his mama never had the heart to tell him not to.

☞ Bites his fingernails and spits them across the room because his mama never had the heart to tell him not to.

☞ Is as rigid as a baby in his routines (i.e. has absolute set times when he needs to eat, or he turns ugly).

☞ Has trouble in general rolling with the flow. Does not like ambiguity.

☞ Needs time to stay out playing with his friends.

☞ Has strong likes and dislikes in food and drink (i.e. your basic meat and potatoes man). Alcoholic beverage of choice: beer.

☞ Has powerful regional loyalties to his town, his state, his school, and probably his favorite football team. Also to his friends and family.

☞ Is usually a hard worker. (Beware the mama's boy who can't seem to find his calling in life.)

☛ Always does what he says he will do. Has a strong belief in honor. Tends to be conservative in his political views, but tolerant and kind to people as individuals.

☛ Has strong pride in his masculinity. Does not cotton to artistic experiences or events such as the ballet, symphony, or art openings.

Generally speaking, the mama-dependent, while fully capable of being obnoxious and even intolerable to the point of boorishness, has a certain basic niceness to him and a natural generosity that, with the proper encouragement, can blossom into a lifetime of tender love and caring. Depending on how mama-influenced he is, roping him in can be as easy as shooting fish in a barrel. So like I said earlier, be careful! If this is not the man for you, back off. It's all too easy for an impulsive, love-hungry Cowgirl to get stuck with the wrong kind of guy. Just because he's eager, you're eager, and he's convenient, doesn't make him right.

Now let's take a look at the counterpart of our mama's boy, the mama-deprived man.

This is the male who is the product of an absent mama. Why has mama been absent? Any number of reasons. Classic cases include the mama who is subject to nervous problems or depression and is, to say the least, in need of rather frequent medication. Your basic swooner or victim of what in the old days they used to call the vapors.

It's also possible that mama was highly repressed. She never fit the Calamity Jane (nurturer) mold, and yet was forced into it by the traditions of culture. She did what was expected of her and was never emotionally available to her son.

Or she may have died young, when our poor boy was yet a babe.

Then you have the wild-woman mama. This one didn't even pretend to do what was expected of her. She stayed drunk or gone or crazy or whatever and her little baby boy never did see enough of her.

There can be any number of reasons why mama neglected her boy. No doubt she loved him but she never did show it, or know how to show it. As a result, she produced archetypal male Number Two: the mama-deprived. He is the one who is consistently attracted to women who are unattainable, just like mama. Here's how to recognize him:

The Mama-Deprived Male

- Is more likely to have lived in various regions of the United States at one time or another.

- Is likely to have accomplished, or be striving to accomplish, great things in the world to make up for the fact that his mother neglected him.

- Thrives on ambiguity and the unexpected. Rarely appears or call when he says he will; likes to play things by ear and make plans at the last minute.

- Highly romantic when he chooses to be. Likes candlelit dinners, sends roses. Knows his wines.

- Has an elegant wardrobe; dresses and grooms well. (However, take note that it's also possible for this man to be a slob who looks ruggedly attractive even at his worst.)

- Has impeccable manners. May be a hand-kisser.

- Typically has a highly developed sense of culture and good taste. Loves beautiful things, actually enjoys and will accompany you to concerts, art shows, and other cultural events.

- Tends to be more liberal in his political views. Shows great consideration to strangers, but is less than generous with those close to him.

- Needs a lot of time alone. May be a fly fisherman, sculptor, musician, birdwatcher, or other solitary, sensitive type. Many so-called horse whisperers fit this profile. (Warning: avoid writers and house-painters.)

- Has eclectic culinary tastes. Likes spicy food and will actually eat (or try) exotic cuisines. May even be a champagne drinker.

Generally speaking, the mama-deprived has a tendency to appear caring and even loving on the surface, due to his innate natural charm. Be warned. This man is often extremely self-involved, selfish, inconsiderate, and even downright mean when you scratch the surface. He will be a more difficult catch and, if you marry him, may take a lot of work before he is even in the trainable category of civilized domestic relations.

CHAPTER FOUR

The Daddy Factor

John Wayne is as John Wayne does.
— Aunt Patricia "Pete" Davidson

Although the Mama Factor is the key to understanding and captivating your man, the Daddy
Factor plays its own role in your grasp of both his
nature and yours.

The basic premise is twofold. One, most men
tend to be just like their Daddies. If you want to
know from whence your man came, where he's at,
and where he's going, just take a look at his
Daddy. If Daddy likes to sit in a duckblind all day,
drink whiskey, and root for his favorite team, so
will your sweet John Wayne. If Daddy is a sales-
man who has spent his life retailing cheap men's
suits – Johnnie-Boy will do likewise. He may sell
cars or real estate or pharmaceuticals instead of
suits, but you get the idea.

If Daddy is a symphony conductor who has
married and divorced three times and collects
Wedgwood, your cowboy probably at least plays in
a band, is likely to be somewhat of a philanderer,
and collects folk art.

The point of the first half of our Daddy Factor
premise? To know your man, find out everything
you can (discreetly) about his Daddy. (You'd want
to know everything you could about the sire of
your horse, right?)You might argue that this goes
against our earlier premise that men are defined by
the nature of their mother conflict, a.k.a. The
Mama Factor. Actually, it's just another way of
looking at The Mama Factor. Just think about it –
if your cowboy's Daddy married an unattainable

woman, it's because he is the son of one. If his Daddy married a nurturer, it's because he is the son of one. And so on back into history for time immemorial, the matriarch has controlled the universe and all of society.

So let's move on to the second half of our premise: your own Daddy. Let's face it, when we girls go looking for a mate, we tend to look for the characteristics we're so familiar with in our own Daddies. So take a long look at your own Daddy and try to decide what you really love about him, and what you could do without.

Do you love his loyalty and reliability, but could do without his rigid insistence on certain routines and refusal to eat anything other than meat and potatoes? Then you want the basic mama-dependent man, but toned down to a considerable degree. (We'll talk in the next chapter about toning down or gearing up to type.)

Do you admire the way your Daddy scorns the mushy and sentimental, knows everything about opera, looks great in a tux, and likes to frequent fancy restaurants? But you hate the fact that he has never told you he loves you and seems terrified of any kind of intimate conversation? Then your Daddy is a mama-deprived, for sure, and that's probably the type of man for you. But you want a mama-deprived who has had some feeling for others knocked into him somewhere along the way.

One thing you must never, never expect: that

you will be able to change your man. John Wayne is as John Wayne does. It has always been that way and always will be. That's why you must be sure you have set your sights on what you want before you apply your Cowgirl Code full strength.

You must admit, it would have been a disaster if Annie Oakley had married a hot-looking but terminally button-down traditionalist banker or farmer (like her Dad) instead of the wonderful Frank Butler, a fellow sharp-shooter who became not only her husband and soul mate, but also her manager. Together they traveled the world, doing things another man might have given Annie considerable grief about. Let's face it, another man would most likely have wanted to change Annie Oakley, which would have drained the happiness from her life.

Annie was an exception to the rule, especially for her day. More common were domestic partnerships like the one Calamity Jane and her husband, Clinton Burke, had. Calamity (real name: Martha Jane Canary) was orphaned when she was young, and spent her life wandering the frontier rescuing people from desperate situations. Maybe because she was an orphan who never really had anyone to love and take care of her, she had this strong desire to do for others. Maybe that's why she married a kind of father figure in Mr. Burke. Anyway, it didn't work out. The guy deserted her early on. Calamity just kept on with her life as she had always known it.

Or take Lucille Mulhall, the amazing lady who's pretty much recognized as the world's first official Cowgirl. This soft-looking, sweet-talking, highly educated and very feminine little Oklahoma girl could have been a maven of early twentieth-century high society, and a model of the traditional woman of her day. But her heart called her to the outdoors. From the time she was a little girl, she knew she would rather be riding and roping than sipping tea with her little finger in the air. Women weren't exactly accepted out on the range in those days, so Lucille took to show business, rodeo-style. She was the talk of Manhattan when she appeared at Madison Square Garden in 1905, and legend has it that President Teddy Roosevelt coined the word "Cowgirl" to describe our gal.

Lucille Mulhall never stopped pursuing her first love – horses and the rodeo – her entire life. Unfortunately, like a lot of us Cowgirls, she made a few bad choices in her personal life. Guys who couldn't figure out why she wouldn't settle down and stay home to cook and clean. So Lucille's two marriages both ended in divorce. Now if only Lucille had picked more appropriate romantic pardners, like Annie Oakley did, maybe she would have been a lot happier.

Times are supposed to be different now, but you still see a lot of heartbreak resulting from Cowgirls marrying the wrong man for the wrong reasons.

Don't let that mistake happen to you! You are who you are, Cowgirl, and if your personal John Wayne is not a fit, you're never going to find the happiness you deserve. Like my Aunt Pete says, the pasture is full of pretty horses. Checking out both the Mama Factor and the Daddy Factor before you get too involved with any one particular animal is part of your Cowgirl Insurance Policy against heartbreak, along whatever trail you follow.

CHAPTER FIVE

Fully Understanding John Wayne

Why leave the nut you got for one you don't know?

— Loretta Lynn

At this point you should have an idea of whether you type as a Calamity Jane, Lady Godiva, or Annie Oakley, and whether the right man for you falls into the category of mama-dependent or mama-deprived. You have confirmed his tendencies and yours by checking out the Daddy Factor, and are ready to refine your understanding of your darling future mate and trail pardner whom I like to call John Wayne.

Remember, knowledge conquers all – a secret known by Cowgirls that somehow, over the ages, has managed to elude cowboys. This is as it should be. Too much knowledge confuses the cowboy and, when he is confused, he tends to run away or act like a fussy baby (which, of course, you don't want him to do).

Just in case you've been asleep for most of your life, trapped underground, or held hostage in a convent, the following checklist will help you further your understanding of your man by filling you in on some tendencies common to all red-blooded American cowboys – be they the urban, suburban, or dirt-lot rodeo variation on the species.

Basic John Wayne

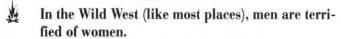 In the Wild West (like most places), men are terrified of women.

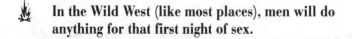 In the Wild West (like most places), men will do anything for that first night of sex.

🌵 In the Wild West (like most places), men don't talk to each other about their emotional involvement with the opposite sex. (Well, at least not honestly.)

🌵 In the Wild West (like most places), men truly do want more than just a shallow relationship with no phone calls and lots of sex. They just think that's all they want.

🌵 In the Wild West (like most places), men will expect you to take an interest in their hobbies and pursuits, but will rarely take an interest in yours (unless you require that they do).

What are you supposed to do with this information now that you have it? It's all designed to help you manipulate John Wayne to your ends. And he doesn't know it yet, but once you have achieved the latter, he will be happier for it, too. Just like a well-trained horse. Let's take it point by point:

1. Men are terrified of women because they are afraid of power they don't understand. Their fear is the simple reason why men don't call. It's why it is so hard for them to get around to asking you out in the first place. And it's why they are afraid to make a gesture such as sending flowers or a note or even a fresh possum steak. They are just plain scared little boys who aren't sure how you (the surrogate mama) will react. And of course, in a mama-dominated society, how mama reacts determines whether the sun will rise or not. Whether baby

Johnny-Boy Wayne will live or die.

2. Where you have him is this: you are a poten-
tial sexual partner; mama is not. (Or let's hope
not.) Thus, the source of woman's power over man.
He'll do anything for it so it only follows that to
keep him doing anything, you need to withhold it
for as long as possible. (More about this in Chapter
Ten.) And let's not forget that you have your honor
to consider. Yes, I said honor.

3. You can safely assume that John Wayne is
not sitting at home or with his friends weaving
elaborate schemes to "get" you the way that you
might be doing to get him. Mr. Wayne, I'm afraid
to say, does not think in those terms. In fact he
does not think at all about you. He may feel a
want, a need, an attraction, but he does not analyze
it, he does not pick it apart during sleepover parties
with his guy friends, he does not ask others their
advice on how to captivate your heart, he does not
even ask himself this stuff. He simply wants, he
needs, he acts. Most important, he reacts – to you.
So you must be careful with your behavior.
Don't get me wrong; I am not telling you to play
games or fake it in order to snare a man. Why
would you want such a man in the first place? I'm
telling you that men have basic buttons that, once
pushed, give you a certain result. If you push the
wrong one without thinking, you could end up with

your life in a mess. And the goal here is to control your life. For example, if you have a flirtatious personality, your teasing could accidentally snag you a mama-deprived who will be emotionally aloof in the long run. Not good if you are a Calamity Jane who really needs a tender, cuddly mama-dependent in her life. This may sound complicated, but it's easy if you just remember one simple rule: Look before you leap! A cowgirl never wants to end up on the back of a runaway horse, but you will if you don't maintain control of the reins.

4. One thing John Wayne does want that he may not know he wants is stability. A wife and a home are the one sure way to get that stability. Whether he's a mama-dependent or a mama-deprived, he needs someone to take care of him. I use that phrase very loosely. You must know that your success in catching your man, and your success in managing him after marriage, all will lie in the WAY you take care of him, and vice versa. You could, with a mama-deprived, be taking care of your man without appearing to be doing anything at all. And vice versa.

5. Face the fact. John Wayne will expect you to be as interested in the Dow Jones Averages, the Talladega 500, or the Bassmasters Classic as he is. Face another fact. You're going to have to either be interested, pretend to be interested, or get interested.

I strongly recommend not pretending. You won't be happy in the long run in any relationship if you can't be yourself. If you share interests, great. If you don't, and don't want to, that's OK, too. But if, like most of us, you are somewhere in between, your guy should give to you as much as he expects to get. If your interests are so different that you can't find a bridge between the two of you, well you're probably in trouble. This guy is probably not a lifetime ride unless you actually want and need a life that is separate, to a considerable degree, from your mate's.

Now for some additional factors that will help you fully identify and understand your ideal mama-dependent or mama-deprived man:

Circumstances that Mediate the Mama Factor

- Number of children in his family and his position in the line-up.

- If his mama was absent, whether there was a surrogate mama figure who raised him.

- Whether he had sisters, how many, and their relative positions to him in the line-up.

- If he was adopted.

- If his Daddy has passed away, how young Johnny-Boy was when it happened.

WARNING:
Things You Might Be Fooled into Thinking Mediate the Mama Factor, But Don't

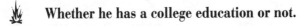

- Whether he has a college education or not.

- His chosen job or profession.

- Whether he has lived outside his home state.

- How well-traveled he is generally.

- His political views.

- Whether he has been in therapy.

- How macho he appears on the surface.

- How smart he is.

It's important that you listen real good here, because you easily can be fooled by a man, especially a cowboy, especially a real charming cowboy, into thinking the Mama Factor has been mediated or even alleviated by a long list of worldly factors. This is, as my dear old great Aunt Sally used to say, bull tweedie.

The only thing that can tone down (or intensify) the Mama Factor are family circumstances that came into the picture long before you did. You can't do anything about them, so don't even try. If, after looking at his family makeup and fully understanding your John Wayne, you decide he isn't

right for you, have the courage to end the relationship and move on. You cannot change a man.
Especially a cowboy. And NEVER FORGET: They
are all cowboys.

That said, let's take the mediating factors one
by one:

1. The number of children in his family is critical.
An only male child, be he mama-dependent or
mama-deprived, will represent the strongest, most
unmitigated specimen available of his type. In
other words, if his mama was a smothering mama
and he was her only child, look out. You got an
extra-strength mama-dependent on your hands.

If his mama was an absent mama and he was
her only child, look out. You got an extra-strength
mama-deprived on your hands. Both, by the way,
are the biggest kind of babies.

On the other hand, the more children there
were in his family, the more mama's influence is
mitigated. A mama-dependent type from a family
of eight children is much more likely to be his own
man, malleable and more mature, than a mama-
dependent from a smaller family or an only-child
family. Same thing goes for your mama-deprived
types. Bottom line: If you fall between types, you
want a man who falls between types. That kind of
man is more likely to have come from a mama who
gave him some siblings. So that, in other words, the
poor fellow had a prayer of being socialized to

some normal extent.

One word of caution here: If your man is from a large family but is the oldest or youngest, he may still suffer from only-child syndrome because, either way, he could have spent a great deal of time either alone with mama or under her intense influence.

2. A surrogate mama can go a certain distance, sometimes a long way, in counteracting either the claustrophobic mama or the unavailable mama. In the good (?) old days, this was a benefit of the now nearly extinct domestic servant system. It is not the purpose of this book to pass judgment either way on this system. But the fact remains that many men now in their thirties and older had a maid, be she black, white, red, or yellow, who played a critical role in their upbringing. Not infrequently, these domestic employees brought a certain breadth of world view to the otherwise suffocatingly mama-dependent child's world; or, on the other side of the coin, taught the abjectly lonely mama-deprived child how to love. Naturally, such surrogate mother relationships are rarely so clear cut. But you get the point. They can serve to mediate the Mama Factor.

Other surrogate mothering, to the same effect, may come from a live-in aunt, grandmother, or even an older sister (see next point).

3. If your John Wayne had a sister or sisters, he is going to be more well-rounded than the only child

mama-dependent or mama-deprived, or than the latter who comes from a family of brothers.

4. If Johnny-Boy was adopted, the Mama Factor and all other factors generally apply, especially if he was adopted as a baby. If he was adopted later than that, there's no telling.

5. If Johnny's Daddy has passed, especially if he passed while Johnny-Boy was quite young, the Mama Factor will be strengthened. This also applies if Mama and Daddy were divorced (with mama retaining custody) while our boy was young.

CHAPTER SIX

A Footnote on Avoiding the New-Age Cowboy

*Deja Moo: The feeling that you've
heard this bull before.*

— Unknown

Girls, we'd all like to think that after "X" amount of therapy, and "X" amount of time working for the Peace Corps or Greenpeace or the local recycling center, and "X" amount of time in search of root chakra, not to mention "X" number of hours of ass-busting physical and mental trail riding, such cultural phenomena as the Mama Factor might fizzle out, lose their potency, and disappear from the human emotional and psychological landscape altogether.

Not so.

Don't make the mistake of thinking so. You will find yourself breaking the rules and losing your man before you can say, "Green Tea."

I strongly counsel you to avoid the New-Age Male, especially the New-Age Cowboy, because he isn't real. He is someone pretending to be someone else. Is that the kind of person you want to spend the rest of your life with?

If your man doesn't know who he is and doesn't accept himself at this point, honey, you're lost and so is he.

To help you recognize the New-Age Cowboy on the trail and avoid him before you find yourself wasting your precious time on him, here are a few key identifiers:

Field Guide to the New-Age Cowboy

 Claims to have numerous female acquaintances who are "just friends."

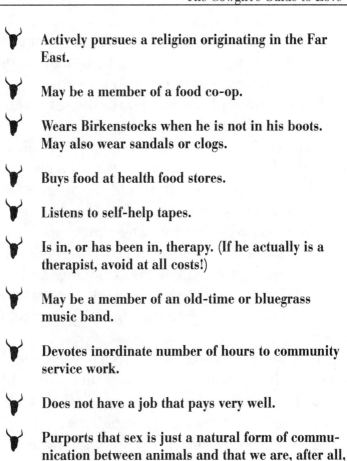

- Actively pursues a religion originating in the Far East.

- May be a member of a food co-op.

- Wears Birkenstocks when he is not in his boots. May also wear sandals or clogs.

- Buys food at health food stores.

- Listens to self-help tapes.

- Is in, or has been in, therapy. (If he actually is a therapist, avoid at all costs!)

- May be a member of an old-time or bluegrass music band.

- Devotes inordinate number of hours to community service work.

- Does not have a job that pays very well.

- Purports that sex is just a natural form of communication between animals and that we are, after all, animals.

- Claims to feel more comfortable with women than with men.

This guy is just plain more trouble than he's worth. Because you are the Queen of the Rodeo, you deserve the Cowboy of your Dreams. A real man! Not some bum in sandals. Do yourself a favor and don't even think about investing your valuable time in this pretender. Once you get through all the smoke and mirrors, you're just going to have to deal with the Mama Factor anyway. Might as well start right off there to begin with.

I wish that is what my friend, Becky, had done, instead of falling into a relationship with a classic New-Age Cowboy I will call Arnold. Becky was feeling vulnerable after breaking up with her demanding mama's-boy of a fiance. She was spending a lot of time working her feelings out on horseback, riding the trail or just grooming and being with her horse. So when Arnold came on the scene as the new manager at the barn where Becky stabled, it was all over.

At first blush, Arnold looked to be everything that old boyfriend wasn't: easygoing, nurturing, in touch with his own feelings, concerned about and supportive of hers. Becky and Arnold started to ride together on a regular basis, talking for hours as they did. Arnold was in therapy after separating from his wife and knew all the right buzzwords. He encouraged Becky to follow her heart, process her grief, and get in touch with herself. He suggested she forgive her mother for ancient wrongdoings, and re-establish contact with her long-absent father. He told her all this would be good for her head. Arnold let it be known that he used to make big money selling pharmaceuticals, but had quit in favor of full-time life in the horse world, because the business was too shallow and demoralizing for him. He believed everyone should live in the moment, and just do what they really wanted to do. Oh boy, the perfect (NOT) man!

Turned out that for Arnold, living in the moment required him to borrow money from Beck now and then. It seemed to involve some bouts with drinking and those pharmaceuticals that he no longer sold, but apparently still had ready access to. Turns out that when Becky wasn't around to watch, he was mean to his horse. Beck started to get a bad feeling and to back away from Arnold, which, of course, only caused him to pursue her harder. He got obsessive, calling her at all hours dozens of times a day and even pressing a new cell phone on her especially for him to call on. By then she wanted nothing to do with him, but by then, it was too late – he was stalking her: parking outside her old boyfriend's house thinking she might show up; parking outside her office and waiting for her to get off work. He even followed her to the gyne- cologist, and accused her of having an affair with her doctor.

Good thing Arnold's wife (with whom he still lived, after all) finally had the cops pick him up and then packed him off to some dry-out facility. After that, Becky heard he went to jail for selling pills. In the end, old Arnold was nothing but a big fat mama-deprived looking for someone to take it all out on. Thank goodness, Becky got out of that.

CHAPTER SEVEN

Strategizing for the Mama Factor

Cowgirl: A better looking cowboy with brains.

— *Unknown*

Your basic strategy is simple. You must, more or less, replicate his mama. OK, before you gag and throw-up, give me a chance to explain.

First of all, let me say that if replicating his mama does not jibe with your natural tendencies, then you've got the wrong guy to begin with. So what I'm really telling you is to be yourself (a Cowgirl never fakes who she is), but with an extra added level of self-awareness as well as a special radar for his actions and sensibilities. Don't tell me you don't think about this stuff, even obsess about it, especially when you're snugged up with your cowgirl friends talking about your men, as we all love to do. Did I make him mad? Why didn't he call me back? Should I ask him to do this or that, or not? For all those times when you wonder and feel unsure of yourself, like I said earlier in this book, *listen to your Inner Cowgirl*. She's gonna tell you that on the trail of life happiness, romance, and fulfillment, you gotta know how to read the signs and act accordingly. If you don't take charge of your own happiness, no one else will. And face it, strategizing for the Mama Factor is part of the deal.

So. If your man is a mama-dependent, you have the opportunity to realize happiness by plying your homemaking skills. If he is mama-deprived, it's OK to distance yourself without worrying about chasing him away, because that behavior works for both of you.

Remember that you must do all this within the basic context of living your very, very busy Cowgirl Life. A true Cowgirl is always busy and in high demand. She has pals who need her friendship and chores around the ranch. She has to spend lots of time getting ready to look good and ride well at the rodeo. There's no end of things for her to do. Because a Cowgirl is someone *who has a life, with or without a man*. If that doesn't describe you, girl, you need to do something about it. Forget about mating for right now and find something else to be interested in. Do volunteer work, save hurt animals, join the gym, start a book club, take up knitting, anything that interests you! If you don't have a busy life, you are way too needy and dependent to make a happy relationship with anybody. You'll just end up with a loser who is even more needy and dependent than you. Ugh!

So point made, I hope. You have a life, and that means you are not revolving around a man like a planet around the sun. But you do want to strategize to make him happy and win his heart, just as you would to keep your horse loyal and loving, obedient and well-rewarded – the perfect long-term partner on the trail.

Thus, domestic bliss will make the mama-dependent happy. But don't go overboard. Just because your man is mama-dependent doesn't mean you should chase after him with a pot of chicken soup and a fresh-baked apple pie. No, you just want to have these things around, and have them be fabulous, when he comes over for dinner. Because that is what *you* enjoy, too.

By the same token, just because your man is mama-deprived doesn't mean you can't give him little gifts or make suggestions that will help him. Just do it in a very unsentimental way, and do it infrequently – after he's done something for you first.

Here are some basic pointers. Remember, if two or more of these points turn you off, a mama-dependent man is probably not the right type for you.

How to Manage Mama-Dependent John Wayne

Don't forget, first and foremost, you are the Queen of the Rodeo. He is, at least at first, just someone to dance with. You lived without other men, and you can live without him.

If he is mama-dependent, he will be dazzled by proficient domestic skills. However, you mustn't overdo this stuff unless it's what you really want to do – unless it makes you happy, too.

If you often have delicious homemade snacks on hand, so much the better.

A delicious home-cooked dinner will go a long way, but don't push this too hard too soon. Let it take place in its own good time, no sooner than the third date.

- If he leaves items of clothing at your house (don't encourage this), return them promptly, washed and pressed.

- If he offers an opportunity to meet his family, accept graciously and behave graciously.

- When the opportunity arises, take him on a sumptuous picnic (prepared by you, of course.)

- When you are at his place, always clean up tidily after yourself, and leave the place a little cleaner overall then when you arrived.

- Make an effort to get along well with his horse and/or other pets (which, if he is mama-dependent, he is likely to have).

- As the opportunity arises, indulge your innate urge to please his parents and siblings by doing or making things for them.

If the following guidelines for managing the mama-deprived feel more like your style, well, that should tell you something.

How to Manage Mama-Deprived John Wayne

- Always remember, first and foremost, you are the Queen of the Rodeo. He is, at least at first, just someone to dance with. You lived without other men, and you can live without him.

- If he is mama-deprived, he will be alarmed by too much domesticity. It is something unfamiliar that he doesn't know how to deal with. Assuming you have decided that a mama-deprived is right for you, you can comfortably follow your instinct to not vacuum the house or bake a pie before he comes over.

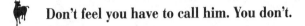 It is perfectly all right not to bend over backward in any overt, traditionally female way for this man.

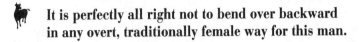 Don't feel you have to call him. You don't.

Don't feel you have to cook for him. If you eat at your place, order out.

If you have dinner together, a restaurant is the best suggestion. Don't suggest your place or his unless he does. Let him pay.

If he offers an opportunity to meet members of his family, find a way to politely, but credibly, beg off or postpone this occurrence.

Avoid independently contacting members of his family, or any attempts to get close to him through his family. A card at Christmas is enough.

He will probably not have house pets. If he does, they will be cats. Ignore them.

Don't drop hints about gifts you'd like for your birthday, Valentine's Day, or Christmas. Be silent. If he gives you something, accept it with a polite "thank you."

One final word of caution. When I give you male-management tips, I mean them always within the context of the Cowgirl Code. That is, never "chase" a man. Never EVER beg. That sort of thing is pure-dee beneath you. It will instantly kill the mystery for both of you (not to mention tainting your sense of honor and dignity). The guy either likes you or he doesn't. If he does, and you like him, that's when all these hints and tips come in handy. If he doesn't like you, that's his problem. Don't let it be yours. A Cowgirl always has lots of other friends and admirers, and plenty to do to keep her busy. She doesn't waste her time designing on some loser who doesn't appreciate her.

CHAPTER EIGHT

That First Date: Reining Techniques

When choosing between two evils, I always like to try the ones I've never tried before.
— *Mae West*

For you Cowgirls who have never been on a horse before, "reining technique" is that subtle set of skills that allows you to manipulate your reins in such a way as to direct the ride to the destination of your choice, along the route of your choice, and at the pace of your choice. You might, if you are very skilled, even get your horse to do some tricks along the way.

Knowing just how to flick the reins on a first date is something you know whether you realize it or not. You were born with these skills, just like you were born with female hormones that gave you a taste for chocolate and firelight. With the help of your natural inborn reining techniques, that first date should be a magical event, if he is the man for you. When you look back on it, there should be sparkles all around it. You should float home on a cloud, and everyone who looks at you will be able to see the glow.

It doesn't always happen this way. Just like a horse can turn out to be the wrong ride for you, the same thing can happen with a man. On a first date, more often than not that is the case. But when you feel that special something about a cowboy, and you want to make sure that first date goes exactly right... well, it's so easy it's almost embarrassing to have to write it down. But for the sake of future generations who might never have heard of a Cowgirl, or heard Patsy Montana sing, here's how it's done:

First-Date Tips

🐃 Wear something that makes you feel special and secure in yourself, even if it is just a lucky scarf or pin.

🐃 To whatever extent is within your power, encourage the date to take place in a scenario that suits your persona: if you're the more elegant or Rhinestone type of Cowgirl, over dinner in a nice place where you can bring to bear the full power of your hair, makeup, and wardrobe (vs. a hiking expedition or day of fishing); or if you are a real rough rider most comfortable with a sunburn across the bridge of your nose, go for that outdoor expedition. Bottom line: Don't just blindly agree to do whatever he suggests.

🐃 Don't drink too much. No one is attracted to a sloppy woman.

🐃 Don't eat too much. Overeating will make you sleepy and dull and besides, you'll hate yourself later.

🐃 Be the first one to initiate the termination of the date. (A Cowgirl always wants to maintain control of the reins.)

🐃 If he drives you home, let him walk you to the door, but stop him there. (A Cowgirl always wants to maintain control of the reins.)

🐃 Don't kiss him except in a friendly manner, on the cheek, or with closed mouth on the lips. (A Cowgirl always wants to maintain control of the reins. Are you getting this?)

🐃 Don't ask him to call you. If he asks if he can call
   you again, agree politely.

🐃 Never forget how fortunate this man is that you
   have agreed to grace his life with your charming
   company.

🐃 If you never hear from him again, so be it. Move on.

Sometimes, the best way to illustrate a point is
to show what not to do. I can't think of a better
example of this than my cousin, Cheryl. I lived for
awhile with Cheryl in her house outside Salt Lake
City, Utah, during the time that she was trying to
recover from her breakup with a man she cohabi-
tated with for 18 years. Cheryl is a first-rate
Cowgirl and all-around outdoorswoman. She trains
horses, she flies planes, she skydives and hang-
glides, and she works part-time in the summer as a
whitewater raft guide on the Colorado River. You
would think this girl would have a grain of sense.
   But no. She picked 18 years of misery over the
alternative, and it all got its start on the first date.
The guy's name was Larry. She met him on a raft-
ing trip, they had a first date, he spent the night at
her house, and he basically never went home. It's
not like Cheryl couldn't see plain as day that Larry
was a jerk. He didn't have any money, he dressed
like a slob, he drank all her beer, he whined and
cried until she agreed to sleep with him, and then
he wouldn't leave.

Poor Cheryl, not being too sharp on her reining skills, didn't know what to do. So she did nothing. They lived together for 18 years. Here's how she finally broke it off: One time when Larry was over at his mother's (where he'd lived until he moved in on Cheryl), she packed up her stuff and just moved to a rental house on the outskirts of town. That's where she was living when I stayed with her. Larry was still in her house in town where, as far as I know, he is living to this day, with Cheryl paying for it. I guess she's afraid that if she tries to kick him out of there, he'll move in with her at the rented house, and then she'll be back where she started. What a mess. You got to nip that kind of thing in the bud.

CHAPTER NINE

Trailriding Tips (Keep Sex Out of It, and Conserve Ammunition)

*I hope people realize there is a brain underneath
the hair and a heart underneath the boobs.*
                                        — *Dolly Parton*

Many of you are not going to like this part of the Cowgirl's Guide, but I have to be very forceful in telling you that this material lies at the heart of the matter. So pay attention.

How do you think women have controlled their men from time immemorial? The judicious granting of one's physical affections is not to be taken lightly, and is a rule not to be violated if you hope to win your man and keep him. *And* hang onto your own self-respect (the key ingredient in every Cowgirl's magic medicine bag)! Quite frankly, there's no priority more important: the little matter of your own self-worth. Cowgirls simply do not throw themselves away. Cowgirls guard their Preciousness like gold. Cowgirls are not cattle; they are not some commodity to be used up and discarded. They are the Best, Most Useful, Caring, and Fun-Loving People on Earth. They are the opposite of tramps. They might have a lot of fun acting a little trampy now and then, but honey that is a far cry from throwing yourself in the bunk just so some guy will like you. Never forget this!

The single most important part of the Cowgirl Code is that you absolutely should never have sex on the first date, and certainly never ever until you know for sure that he loves you and vice versa. Preferably wait until you are at least going steady.

Sorry, I know you don't like it. It's old-fashioned, it isn't the way the world is any more, it's *uncool*. Uh-unh. You're uncool if you don't get this.

Just think about how many shack-ups don't work out in the end. Why do you suppose that is? It's because boundaries are critical to successful relationships, be they between woman and horse or woman and man. Without boundaries, things turn into a mess. Respect is also critical to every successful relationship. So is the reward system.

He won't respect you if you give him sex too soon. And you won't have any way left of controlling or inducing the behavior you want if you've taken away his incentive. It's like spoiling a child rotten or giving a horse too much sugar for no good reason other than you don't think enough of yourself to relate on a higher plane with others. That is: you don't know how to say "no."

There you have it. Control yourself. Do whatever you have to do. But let no man have any before his time. If that chases him away, he was not the man for you. He will never love or respect you anyway, so you've lost nothing.

You'll also find, if you haven't already, that in a romantic relationship, sex changes everything. Not necessarily for the man, but for the woman. John Wayne will still go along being the same old cowboy whether he gets you into bed or not. He certainly won't think any more of you by getting you into bed, you can be sure of that.

But the moment you have gone to bed with him, especially if you do it too soon, you'll start thinking differently about him, *and* about yourself.

Your thinking will get fuzzy. You stand a very good chance of acting needy and sentimental. You'll have a hard time analyzing the situation clearly, doing the right thing, and drawing the necessary boundaries. Next thing you know, you've broken the Cowgirl Code, along with your heart.

Take my word for it and protect yourself! Don't let John Wayne, no matter how great you think he is, take away your sense of Who You Are. Keep your Sacred Font holy, until Johnny-Boy has proven himself worthy of entry into the chapel of love.

Ten Things to Do Instead of Having Sex

- Eat something rich and sweet.

- Distract him by turning on ESPN.

- Ask him to tell you again about his truck (or horse, or boat, or car).

- Get him to show you the tricks his dog does.

- Suddenly remember you have to get up early to ride your horse or visit your mama.

- Tell him you have to get home to let your dog/cat out.

- Tell him you need your beauty sleep and it's time for him to leave.

- Go for a walk.

☞ Just say "no, thank you."

☞ If you get absolutely positively desperate, tell him this is an inopportune time of the month (but remember – cowgirls avoid discussing their Female Medicine with men).

OK, this is an extreme example, but that's what examples are by definition, right? It's my cousin, Mary Lee. She lives near Bagley, Minn., in a little town called Rosst, population about 1,300. (Yes, Virginia, there are Cowgirls there, too. Just ask anyone who works at the Bagley Western Wear shop.)

Mary Lee is the person who first told me about that *thing* that happens between men and women. I didn't believe it, but later it was confirmed by a little book with a pink cover that my Mama left discreetly on my bed. Anyway, Mary Lee had a pretty healthy libido. As a young teenager, I didn't have a lot of interest in boys; they just seemed like rude beasts to me at the time. I basically wanted them to leave me alone. But Mary Lee was boy-crazy. All she could think about was driving over to Lengby and cruising around looking for boys. Or maybe hitting the hot spot in town, the A&W drive-in, and checking out the action. It didn't hurt that she was beautiful. At the time, I was pudgy and pimply, which may explain my less-than-enthusiastic attitude. We'd get home late at night, and lay in the twin beds in Mary Lee's bedroom, and just talk about boys. Or rather, she'd talk and I'd listen.

By the time she hit her nineteenth birthday, Mary Lee had met the love of her life. She and David were in college together, at Mankato State. He was going to be a science teacher and she was going to be...well, whatever. They got engaged. Next thing you know I'm the maid of honor walking ahead of 21-year-old Mary Lee down the aisle at the Lutheran church across the street from her Daddy's (my uncle's) grocery store. At the reception, out at my uncle's farm, I admired her glittery diamond ring. As soon as I got a chance to take her aside, I whispered the question that was burning in my brain: "What's *it* like?"

Mary Lee surprised me. "What's what like?"

"You know."

"No, what?"

"Doing it."

"You mean sex?" She laughed and informed me that *she and David were waiting for their wedding night.* That she was a virgin. I couldn't believe it. Mary Lee was, in my imagination, the very image of the modern-day sex goddess. For every minute that I wasn't having a clue as to how sex was done or what it was like, I figured she was out there just lapping it up. I was speechless.

Bottom line: Mary Lee and David had enough sex to produce four fabulously handsome and strapping cowboys; they (Mary Lee and David) are now well into middle age and still goosh and moon over each other like teenagers; I know for a fact, because Mary Lee tells me, that their sex is not only still regular, but imaginative and incredible ('course there isn't much else to do on a farm in northern Minnesota in the winter). And *they actually waited until they were married* to do it. Now all this is to say that I don't recommend this plan for everyone. There's a lot to be said for trying out the merchandise before you buy it. The point is, don't waste your most powerful ammunition shooting at mosquitoes. Save it for the big game.

And the other point is, you can be the sexiest thing on the planet and still not have sex. Sometimes that makes you even sexier.

CHAPTER TEN

Like Horse, Like Man: Make Sure the Brakes Work

Needing a man is like needing a parachute. If he isn't there the first time you need him, chances are you won't be needing him again.

— *Unknown*

This chapter is just another reminder to look before you leap. You wouldn't buy a car or truck that wouldn't stop, would you? You certainly wouldn't buy or lease, or even want to ride one time, a horse that would run away with you. So why do so many of us Cowgirls get hooked up with men who drag us into their way of doing things and right on down a path that is wrong for us before we know it? *Because we neglected to check the brakes.* In horseback riding, as in all other aspects of life, it is a good thing to practice saying "no" now and again. Here are a few tips for doing just that:

How to Test His Brakes

Don't let him be the one who always sets the time for your date. Insist on doing so yourself or on a compromise. If this isn't possible, it's better to just be unavailable.

Don't let him be the one who decides on the venue or activity for every date. Again, if this isn't OK with him, you got a big red flag.

Set your own terms for sex! (See the previous chapter!!!)

If he hurts your feelings, tell him. Right then. His reaction will tell you a lot about his qualifications (or lack thereof) as your future trail pardner.

Request politely that he support you in your interests by attending events of your choice, meeting or socializing with people who are important to you, and giving you his considered opinion on matters of importance to you. Score him without mercy on his performance in this department.

Don't ever be afraid to tell him you don't like something or don't want to do it. (But remember, Cowgirls never, EVER cry! At least not over stuff like this.

Don't ever eat or drink anything just because he wants you to.

Don't ever wear anything just because he wants you to (unless you want to, too.)

Don't be afraid to compete against him and win.

When you know you are right, insist on it and don't back down.

When you are proven right, or you win the competition, never apologize.

If he asks you to go steady or marry him, and you are unsure of what to say, JUST SAY NO!

If your old John Wayne reacts poorly to any of the above, well, sorry gal, but he hasn't passed the test of the Cowgirl Code. Get rid of him. His brakes don't work.

CHAPTER ELEVEN

Love Thy Fellow Cowgirl as Thyself

If we cannot find the road to success, we will make one.
— Unknown

Any man, no matter how much you love him, is gonna disappoint you again and again. But as a general rule, there is one thing in life that will always help you find a way to make it through, and that is your fellow Cowgirls. Cherish your friendships with your girlfriends. Make time for them. They are your allies in this bruising life, inside the rodeo ring and out.

If you're like me and my best Cowgirl friends, you don't need to be told this. But just maybe you need to remind yourself every once in awhile, because it's awfully easy to lose sight of. To me, one of the great things about fellow Cowgirls is that it doesn't take much to make us happy. We can make a party out of anything. Next thing you know we all feel better. We're laughing. We feel hope. We have life and love in a little more perspective. If you have a special Cowgirl friend you haven't talked to lately, why don't you pick up the phone and call her? Below are some other ideas, gleaned from some of my favorite things to do with my girlfriends on Saturday nights:

Girlfriend Stuff

- Build a fire and just sit watching it.

- Get dressed up and go absolutely nowhere.

- Get dressed up and go parade yourself around town. Lead a few men on, and then dismiss them, as you have more important things to do.

- Eat something totally, fabulously delicious.

- Wear hats and/or smoke those little cigars.

- Build a fire and throw into it items symbolic of your romantic disappointments. (An excellent activity on a birthday or at the start of a New Year.)

- Color your hair and/or nails, or help a friend do it.

- Learn to shoot.

- Play poker, blackjack, or any other game that involves a little good-natured, small-time gambling.

- See who can invent the most imaginative cocktail.

I want to tell you a story right here about my Aunt Pete, who lives on a ranch outside of Houston, Texas. I lived with Aunt Pete for awhile when I was in college, or more accurately, during one of those years when I should have been in college but was taking time off to figure things out. I had just endured the first major heartbreak of my life, at the hands of a particularly callous, pseudo-new aged, mama-deprived male. I spent a lot of my time just sitting on the fence out in Aunt Pete's back pasture, gazing at the horizon and pondering Things. Wondering alternately, "What is wrong with me?" and "How could I have been so stupid?" I pondered so much and for so long that I would

sometimes forget what time of day it was or even
what day of the week it was. I was pretty much
digging myself a rut in the middle of nowhere.

Now Aunt Pete is not that type at all (thank
God). This is a woman who, widowed in her early
middle age, lived alone on a hardscrabble ranch
and got along just fine, thank you, with a little help
from a nip of the bottle now and then and the .38
Smith and Wesson revolver she always packed in
the waistband of her jeans. Aunt Pete would have
been in her early seventies around about this time.
You could say she was a Cowgirl of the first caliber,
and always had been all her life. The rest of her
sisters turned into simpering Southern Belles married to bankers and lawyers, but Aunt Pete went
her own way.

My mother, Aunt Pete's younger sister, did
everything she could to get Aunt Pete to lay off me.
For some reason, Mama had the idea that I was a
fragile thing who might break, or have a break-
down, if I was challenged too much. Although she
was an expert horsewoman, Mama was also a mas-
terful society lady who thought if you just didn't
think about a bad thing, put on a pretty dress and
a pair of white gloves, and went to a meeting of the
garden club, everything would be all right – including your marriage to a drunken, out-of-work,
womanizing sot. Mama never got anything more
than half right, poor dear.

Anyway, I'm sitting on the fence, literally and

figuratively, out at Pete's one day when she comes along in her doodlebug, an old VW bug with the back half chopped off and a sheet of plywood slapped on top to make a kind of impromptu flatbed truck. Pete used the doodlebug to haul stuff and tool around her place for whatever general purpose she had. On the flatbed, she had a cooler and a picnic basket. I'm thinking I'm not really in the mood for a picnic, but she surprised me. She jumped out of the 'bug, grabbed the basket and dumped it on the ground in front of me. All of a sudden I'm sitting there looking at five or six pissed-off rattlesnakes. Next thing I know Pete's .38 is in my hand, and I'm shooting the heads off those suckers.

After the snakes were dead, I remember looking down at Pete (I'm not tall, but she was a tiny little thing) with my mouth hanging open and tears streaming down my face before both of us broke into hysterical laughter. "I thought it was about time I showed you what real trouble is like," she snapped. "I thought you needed to know how to deal with it." Well we sat out there on the bed of the doodlebug and drank all 12 beers she had in that cooler before we made our way back to the house for a nice barbecue supper. That bad old man who broke my heart was forgotten, thanks to the intervention of the best Cowgirl friend in the world, Aunt Pete. It just goes to show how important your friends are when it comes to putting things in perspective, giving you the strength to take charge of the situation, and teaching you how to shoot – which I highly recommend as an antidote to any kind of heartbreak.

CHAPTER TWELVE

Meeting the Culhanes

Good friends, food, shade, and tipping our hats
to the American flag...will make any day perfect.
— Cris Paravincini

Meeting your rodeo sweetheart's family is not something you want to think a lot about in advance. If you think too much about it, you'll be too nervous. You'll forget how to act and you might blow it. Plus you'll be so busy worrying about the way you appear to them, that you'll neglect your own important work, which can only take place on this important occasion.

And that is: get a good close look, first-hand, at the Mama who made John Wayne what he is today (not to mention the Daddy and sisters and brothers).

You'll need this information, especially for effective cowboy management after marriage. Watch the way John Wayne relates to his Mama and the way his Mama and Daddy interact. This is what you can expect for you and Johnny-Boy.

Make note of any information Mama imparts as to your cowboy's likes and dislikes, favorite foods, etc. If she's a big-mouth, she'll be likely to let slip some info about your rivals. This is always useful in the way a new horse's ownership history is. (Loretta Lynn summed it up nicely when she said "You have to be first, best, or different.")

The important thing to remember is to be yourself. Sounds obvious, but it is often very hard to do in this particular situation.

Tips for Your First Family Visit

Don't push for this event to happen! It will happen in its own good time.

Don't bring a gift unless you are truly inspired to do so.

Do write a thank-you note afterward, especially if a meal was served.

Don't talk too much!

If questions about your romantic past are asked, be vague.

It goes without saying, but we'll say it anyway: look (translation: feel)your best. Prepare yourself in whatever way you have to so you are comfortable and confident.

Mind your manners. Being yourself doesn't include being rude.

Listen to what others have to say.

Closely observe the family interaction. This is what you'll have on your hands if you marry Johnny-Boy.

Closely observe the individuals themselves. This is a good opportunity for you to decide whether you can live with these people. You surely will be stuck with them, after all, when and if you marry your cowboy sweetheart.

If they hint or ask you outright about your future plans, or any future plans you might have with their baby boy, be vague. You don't owe them any explanations at this point, unless you want to give them.

🎸 If any of the females, Mama in particular, send any
   veiled jabs your way, simply smile sweetly.

🎸 Shake their hands when you are introduced to
   family members, and again upon leaving. It is per-
   missable to give Mama a token hug and an air-kiss.

🎸 Do not discuss politics or religion. The real you can
   let these subjects slide for once.

🎸 A final note on wardrobe. Count on it, you will be
   scored heavily on how you look. And you DO want
   to look fabulous. But by all means, do not dress in
   a flashy or revealing manner. Be sure your clothes
   are modest and in good taste, and that you have on
   sensible shoes or boots in good condition. Mama is
   sure to check out your footwear, and also will draw
   conclusions based on whether your jewelry is
   cheap and flashy, or quiet and tasteful.

My friend, Lucy, is someone I will admire for
the rest of my life after I saw the way she handled a
man who undoubtedly would have busted her precious heart to pieces. Lucy is in the publishing business, and she was dating a highly respected, big-
time publishing executive. This is a man whose
name is known everywhere and we, her best girlfriends, were in awe of her catch. The guy sent her
flowers, took her to exclusive parties, bought her
expensive dinners, and generally made her feel like
the most desirable and beautiful thing on earth. He
would have her over for heavenly weekends at his
brownstone in New York and she would meet us for

lunch afterward with stars in her eyes. She was madly in love (or so she thought) for the first real time in her life, after two failed marriages followed by a string of total losers. The girl was talking about wedding dresses, for heaven's sake.

The problem with Mr. Perfect was that, naturally, he wasn't really perfect. He was just a tiny bit unpredictable. Like she would wait weeks for him to call after one of their weekend shack-ups. He would break dates at the last minute with what, if you had a suspicious mind, could be construed as flimsy excuses. Lucy, of course, was convinced this was all in her mind. Until she met Mr. Perfect's mother.

Lucy actually had the gall to invite herself along to dinner when Perfect tried to wiggle out of a date because his family was in town. Trapped (we now see), he suggested Lucy meet them (his sister and his mother and him) at the Oak Room of the Plaza Hotel. Well, the whole thing was just a disaster. The mother was one of those tight people with a shallow personality, who has spent her life living out a series of bad choices and taking out her resulting misery on everyone around her. She nitpicked and criticized everything about Perfect, from his clothing, to his chosen profession, to his choice of restaurant. She complained that he lived too far away from her to pay enough attention to her (the family was from North Carolina). She actually complained that her late husband had died just to get away from her.

The older sister wasn't much better. A big, grumpy lesbian is how Lucy described her. Apparently, when Perfect was a boy, his Daddy being gone, his care was left in the hands of these neglectful women. Thus, (if you have done your homework with regard to the mama-deprived male) the result was a classic false-front, commitment evasive, discreet but obsessive, womanizing man. He might look like the best catfish in the pond at first. But honey, look out! He's nothing but trouble.

Lucy and I and our other two close girlfriends, Anne and Toni, had spent a lot of hours, candles, and beers formulating our scientific theories regarding the Mama Factor and its influence on the male persona. So our girl Lucy was prepared. She took one look at that bad old Mama, put two and two together, and dumped Mr. Perfect the next day. Of course, that only made him want her more – he pursued her for at least six weeks afterward.

The moral of the story: Don't hesitate to meet the family if the opportunity presents itself. Just don't go into it unprepared.

CHAPTER THIRTEEN

Roll! How Cowgirls Deal with Rejection

*The best cure for a pain in the
butt is to kiss him good-bye.*
— *Gladiola Montana*

Not every man is right for every woman; thus, we go through the world casting each other aside until we make that perfect match. We girls would all like to think that we are always in the position of being the rejector, not the rejectee. But let's face it. No one goes through life without having her heart broken at least once.

Wimpy women may retire to their rooms and weep their lives away when they are rejected, but not us Cowgirls. Oh no. For us, revenge can be a way of life. We live and breathe it, when necessary. The West was built (at least partly) on revenge, and that's a fact that ain't going to change any time soon. So when John Wayne is fool enough to reject you, by all means – SEEK REVENGE!

If you know some bull riders or maybe someone your brother works with who can take him out into a dark alley and do a number on him. . .

Now, now, I was only joking. This man has taken a big enough chunk of your soul with him as it is. You don't want to get tangled up even further on the dark side.

What I mean by seeking revenge is something along the lines of that cliche, "Living well is the best revenge."

First and foremost, you want to do what Cowgirls do whenever they get accidentally thrown by a horse. Tuck your head and roll! Then pick yourself up and dust yourself off. Next thing, if you've been rejected, go straight back to your

Cowgirl Code and remind yourself that, while women are all-purpose creatures, men have a limited range of use in this world. And that's all well and good, but it is NOT worth wasting away over. There are plenty of men available to dance the two-step with you after the rodeo. So go out there right away and get yourself into even better physical shape, even more gorgeous looks, some new clothing – whatever it takes – and get right back out there in the world and go for it.

Your revenge will come, I promise. It will come when that idiotic cowboy who rejected you sees you all aglow on the arm of another man. When he hears that you are engaged to someone far better and more deserving than he. And when he runs into you in a few years at that class reunion or Christmas party and sees what a knockout you still are, even after two kids. He'll see how adoringly your husband gazes at you, as do all the other men in the room, and he'll kick himself with regret for letting you get away.

That, my fellow Cowgirl, is the sweetest revenge we ever get in this life.

So wipe your tears and get your rear end in gear with these helpful hints:

The Cowgirl's Revenge

Allow yourself to cry for twenty minutes at the very most. Any more than that he doesn't deserve, and will make your eyes puffy and unsightly. He doesn't deserve to do that to you, either.

- If it helps you feel better, stick pins in his picture, or doodle on it so he looks ridiculous. You may keep this harmless medicine in sight for a few days, just to remind yourself of what an idiot he is. But put it away after that because, even stuck full of pins and with horns on his head, he doesn't merit that much attention.

- Burn something significantly symbolic of him.

- Allow yourself a drink or two (no more!) if this helps ease the pain. Do not allow yourself to lean on alcohol as a solution to anything.

- Pamper yourself to the absolute ultimate: take long deliciously scented baths; light candles; get a massage and facial; buy yourself something new to wear.

- Take extra good care of your health. Get eight hours of sleep at night; plenty of exercise; eat a balanced diet; take your vitamins.

- Absolutely do not, under any circumstances, call him.

- Do not write him notes or try to get to him through his mama or the rest of his family or friends.

- It is acceptible to appear at social functions you know he will also be attending, as long as you are sure you are fully in control of yourself and can act

**breezy and blase about running into him. Be sure
you are looking fabulous and have a good-looking
date. Otherwise, DON'T GO.**

**Enjoy the company of your fellow Cowgirls, who
will never let you down, and are meant to be called
upon at times like these.**

I have to add a note here that applies specifically to those of you who actually ride horses, and
generally to every girl, rider or not. You already
know this, so it's just a reminder. But when your
heart is broken, there is no better cure than your
horse. Your horse will always love you no matter
what. Even better, you can get up on the back of
your horse and ride! You can ride hard and fast
with the wind in your hair and never look back.
Your horse will take you wherever you want to go,
in your mind and heart and spirit. Not lucky
enough to own or have access to a horse? Try a
bicycle, a motorcycle, a pair of skis. Try your own
two legs and feet. Just get out there and run that
heartbreak right out of your head.

My friend, Toni, took a two-week trail ride
across Texas when her (undeserving) man left her
and she came back 14 pounds thinner, sun-bronzed
and gorgeous, with a big smile on her face and (as
a matter of fact) a new beau in tow.

My other friend, Mary, started walking and did-
n't stop for months. Every day she had off, every

night when she wasn't working, she was out walking, walking, walking. She lost weight and toughened up. She starting taking in injured and homeless animals she found on her travels. She now runs an animal shelter and has decided she is actually happier living alone.

My Aunt Pete, whom I told you about earlier, lost her husband at a relatively young age. She'd known how to ride since she was a child, but when her man died, she taught herself to shoot, and then how to ride and shoot. She's probably won more turkey shoots and made more friends than you and me and all our friends combined, not to mention having saved herself and others (including me) from rattlesnake bites along the way.

CHAPTER FOURTEEN

The Unwashed Factor

A man's gotta do what a man's gotta do.
A woman must do what he can't.
                    — Rhonda Hansome

Friends mean a lot to your darling John Wayne. The stupefying, unmitigated silence of buddies silently fishing the same stream, mutely munching down piles of potato chips while they take in a ball game on TV, the hoisting of a cool one over the usual slaps on the back, complaints about work, and occasional dirty joke are all a mysteriously important, and to Johnny-Boy and his buddies, endlessly fascinating fixture of American male culture.

Let's face it, sometimes your man's buddies stink, either literally or figuratively; hence, the title of this chapter. But whether your man is a mama-dependent or mama-deprived, he will now and always require a certain amount of time off with them doing basically nothing. The role of we females is not to understand this mystery, but to accept it. For Cowboy-Dear, it is not the doing of nothing that is significant, but the fact of just being there. Call it male bonding if you will, although I dislike that new-age term. There is something going on here far deeper and more elemental than a male sensitivity session. In fact it might be more accurate to call it a male insensitivity session.

Whatever you want to call it, the more accepting you are of this, the better your chances of long-term happiness for yourself and your relationship. After all, a Cowgirl doesn't depend on her man being around for happiness. Her man adds to it, for sure. But she makes her happiness herself.

Coping with the Unwashed

∩ Never complain or argue when John Wayne has something to do with his friends.

∩ Act as if you're glad he's going off on his own (you actually are, right?).

∩ Tell him it will be good for him.

∩ Don't ask him what time he'll get home.

∩ The next day or anytime afterward, don't ask him about his male get-together. (You don't really care, right?)

∩ Never ask to go with him.

∩ If he invites you to go, decline.

∩ If his preferred scenario for Unwashed-time is anything that does not involve drinking or hanging out in bars (like grooming horses, building model cars, or playing par-3 golf), by all means encourage it as much as you can. Once you are married, you will want him out of the house and he will need a harmless hobby.

∩ If you haven't already, cultivate your own outside interests that require you to go off from time to time with your own female friends.

∩ If he needs three or more nights out with the Unwashed a week – especially if the nights out revolve around drinking and bars – drop him.

My niece, Paula, reached a watershed with her man a couple of years ago. I remember it well because I was living in the same town at the time, just down the street from them, and it was my shoulder Paula cried on when things went wrong at home. Paula is the Calamity Jane type, the kind of person who thrives on rescuing others. That is no doubt the reason why she married a classic mama-dependent. Her husband, Sid, is a great guy, but flawed like all the rest of them: he drinks a bit too much and sometimes neglects his household responsibilities, basically taking Paula for granted. (Need I point out, she allowed this.)

Well, in addition to being an advertising executive, Sid is also a musician. He plays bass in a bluegrass band. And at least once a week, he would leave home after dinner (assuming he came home at all after work) to hit some bar or other and jam with his buddies. This would all have been just fine with Paula, if Sid could have remembered to give her a little notice, or if he would have just once helped out a little on the home front before he took off with the band, not to return until morning or later. It got to the point where they had such terrible fights every time he wanted to go hang with the guys that Paula would come running up to my place in tears, then spend the night cussing him out. The fights were so bad she was afraid to go home, for fear that when he returned, still riled up, they'd get into it again.

Finally, Paula did what she needed to do. After the routine knock-down-drag-out screaming and yelling match, followed by the bar-destined departure of Sid, she started calmly packing up her and the baby's things. She called a nice mountain inn and made a reservation. When she was ready to go she just sat down and waited for Sid to come home, which he did around dawn in his usual form. Paula then allowed Sid to watch her placidly loading up the car. When he asked where she was going, she simply gave him a beatific smile. He stood there getting increasingly nervous as Paula loaded in the last items, including their baby girl. "Bye-bye," Paula waved sweetly out the window. "See you later." And she drove off. Sid panicked, of course, being the mama-dependent that he is. He was being left alone! Oh my God! Uncertain as to when or if his mama would come back to take care of him! How would he ever manage alone?! He ran pathetically down the street after her van, crying for her to stop, to come back.

Paula and her daughter spent a lovely week in the mountains with another girlfriend and her kids. When she got good and ready, Paula came back. Before that, though, I stopped by just to make sure poor Sid was OK. He was sitting on the porch swing by himself looking like an abandoned puppy. He said he would offer me a beer or something to eat, but there was nothing in the house. Then he started to cry.

Now, when Sid goes to play with the band he helps with dinner first. He always tells Paula where he will be (well most of the time). He still comes home in the wee hours. But Paula can handle it, because she has done whatever she felt like doing while he was out, and had a good time doing it – IF she is even there when he comes home.

CHAPTER FIFTEEN

The Gatorade Factor

You win some, lose some, and wreck some.
— Dale Earnhardt

You can't get away from sports anywhere in this country, unless it is perhaps Maine or the Aleutian Islands. Chances are good, especially if your cowboy is mama-dependent, that he is a sports fan. You can fill in the blank with whatever: football, NASCAR, basketball or baseball. Even if he is mama-deprived, or anywhere in between, he will no doubt be obsessed with some sport. He may be consumed by fishing, or golf, or bowling. Or any combination of one or more sports. (If you are among the luckiest of us, you are a horsewoman whose man shares your passion for what I personally consider to be the most fulfilling of all sports: the breeding, training, and riding of horses. But that's really not a sport; it's a way of life. For the purposes of discussion, I'm setting aside the horse-loving life right now for an analysis of the role of organized, televised, professional and collegiate sports – also known as the Gatorade Factor – in your man's life.)

Your tendency may be to see his chosen televised, media-hyped sport as your rival. Do not make this mistake. His sport is your friend, especially in the long term, when you will see that Johnny needs something to keep him occupied and out of trouble. (See Chapter 14, "The Unwashed Factor.") Sports is the ideal way for Johnny to occupy himself and stay out of trouble. By trouble, I mean drinking and women – the kind of women who hang around bars.

While you want your John Wayne to have his time with the guys, you will also want to be able to participate, at least to the extent of conversing, in his sport. Don't get me wrong. I am not, by any stretch, suggesting you become one of the guys. Quite the contrary. I am suggesting that, to start with, you consider a man whose interests at least partially overlap with yours.

I'm suggesting this for several reasons:

One, you'll need common ground if you're going to manage John Wayne over the long term.

Two, couples who play together stay together.

Three, it will help ease your relations with his family. No doubt, Johnny-Boy's particular sporting interests are shared by his kinfolk. This is especially likely in regard to football and other team loyalties.

Four, as an added fringe benefit, it will give you an edge over other females.

Here are some other important pointers:

Applied Gatorade Science (and other Sports-Related Tips)

🌵 Find out which sports(s) and team(s) he likes.

🌵 Determine the degree of his Gatorade passions. If he has an entire room or other area in his house dedicated to Bear Bryant, Dale Earnhardt, Tiger Woods, or some other sporting icon, drop him. Unless you are equally obsessed with the same demigod. If that is the case, marry him.

❧ If he and a few friends get together an impromptu game of touch football or similar activity, and he invites you to participate, don't do it unless you really, really want to.

❧ If he and a few buddies are getting together to watch the game, either in a public place or one of the guys' houses, and you are invited to participate, don't do it unless you really, really want to. Even then you might not want to.

❧ If he asks you to go with him to a game or event that interests you, by all means go. If you aren't truly interested, by all means don't go.

❧ If he shows up to pick you up for the game with his face painted or wearing a wig in the team colors, stop dating him.

❧ If he gets so violently stressed out in the course of the game, or is so bent out of shape afterward that he scares you, stop dating him.

❧ If he enjoys the game to a sensible degree, does not wear anything outlandish, accepts the outcome of the game for what it is, appears willing to get on with life afterward without ranting and raving, and invites you to a lovely dinner afterward during which he doesn't even bring up the subject of sports, marry him.

❧ There are sports in the world besides football although in the United States many of us do not know this fact. Because sports are so essential to life in this country, you should have at least one sport of your own. Golf and tennis are excellent all-purpose social sports. Billiards is a very sexy game for a woman to excel at. Bowling is fun to do with your girlfriends, and is a great way to meet down-to-earth, blue-collar types. Pick the sport that fits your interests, goals, and aspirations

 And if you really want to turn John Wayne (and yourself) on, get very, very good at it.

CHAPTER SIXTEEN

The Feedbag Factor

*I wish I had time for just one
more bowl of chili.*
   — Kit Carson's last words

For the sake of completing our gospel on dating and mating according to the Cowgirl Code, we must not skip over the Feedbag Factor. After all, a real Cowgirl can do anything (almost) a man can do, but she is also all woman. Putting delicious food on the table is part of that equation for many of us. If the preparation and consumption of food in the company of friends is meaningless to you, skip this chapter. But if food and eating are emotionally and ritualistically woven into the fabric of your social being, your heart, and your soul, as is true of me and my friends, it's worth considering the role that food plays in your romantic relationships.

Feeding the Hungry Cowboy (and Cowgirl)

- Forget this idea that you have to be a good cook, or any kind of a cook, to enjoy a satisfying romantic relationship.

- If you do enjoy cooking, don't feel like you have to be able to cook everything well. Work on cooking a few things well.

- Draw up four or five basic menus that fit a variety of occasions and keep practicing them until you've mastered them.

- Find out what your man's favorite dishes are.

- Find out what his food dislikes are.

- Find out what his snacking habits are. Mama-dependents tend to like the basic stuff, i.e. cookies, chips, and dip; mama-depriveds tend to like the more esoteric items i.e. smoked salmon, brie, grapes.

🐑 Early on in the relationship, you should be able to come to some conclusions based on all this food research. If he won't touch anything more exotic than a green bean, and you are all for adventures in unidentifiable, exotic cuisines, watch out. This sort of thing can be overcome, but it indicates a potentially big personality difference that could make you frustrated and unhappy later on.

🐑 Learn to enjoy the way you serve and eat food as much as the food itself. There's nothing like eating around a campfire, even if you're eating nothing but scorched pork-n-beans.

🐑 In my life, I have found it indispensable to know how to make good bread, pone, or biscuits.

🐑 Breaking bread with someone is a formative experience. It should be a bonding experience and can even be a spiritual or sacred one. Check in with yourself after you've shared your first meal with Mr. Cowboy. Your Inner Cowgirl will tell you whether the experience is a thumbs-up or down. Proceed accordingly.

I have a cautionary tale about the Feedbag Factor and how it can backfire on you. I don't know of any other women who have had this particular experience, but I'm sure they are out there. It involves a boyfriend of mine, a guy I hooked up with on the rebound. Big mistake. Anyway, I

cooked for him on our third or fourth date. Big
home-cooked meal. Fried chicken, mashed potatoes, beans, corn, biscuits, gravy, the whole bit.
Apple pie for dessert. While Number Two was waiting, I put out a platter of snacks. Just the usual
stuff: crackers and cheese, chips and dip, olives and
pickles, I think I had some homemade cheese
straws from my Aunt Pete. So I'm not really looking much at Number Two since I'm busy cooking.
But when the food is all loaded up on the table and
we're ready to eat, I notice that he has cleaned off
the entire snack platter. Like, it is ALL gone, every
last crumb. Wow, I think – the poor guy must be
really hungry.

Now I would have bet you money that after eating our fill of that great big farmhand-type supper,
I would have had enough left for two meals at
least. Nope. Number Two ate it all. IT ALL. With
this scary, almost erotic attention to the food. I
swear, I thought he was going to have an orgasm –
he was making all these smacking and moaning
noises. I chalked it up to an unusually underfed
day on his part; what else was I going to do? Nope
again. A few nights later I cook and, again, he eats
it all. Pretty soon it's a pattern. He comes over and
stands in the pantry making rustling, crunching,
and chomping noises while I cook; then he eats all
the dinner; then he goes back into the pantry for
more. Then he's over at my house while I'm not
home leaving piles of empty cracker and cookie

boxes and crumbs all over the place. Leftovers vanish from the fridge. Next thing you know, he's living at my house and the grocery bill is about to put us out of house and home. When he tried to tell me I wasn't contributing my share of the grocery expenses, I said "enough." That, more or less, was that. Anyway, all this is to say that it is certainly possible to feed a man too well. And if I'd been listening to my Inner Cowgirl instead of acting impulsively, I would have broken it off after that first meal.

CHAPTER SEVENTEEN

More Tools for
Horse Whisperers

*The best way to get a cowboy to do something
is to suggest he is too old for it.*

— *Unknown*

Well, I'm sure that if you haven't seen the movie "The Horse Whisperer," then you have at least heard of it; maybe you've even read the book. Just in case, I'm going to sum up what a horse whisperer is, because I can't think of a better analogy for the way a Cowgirl wants to handle both her horse *and* her man.

The idea is simple. Instead of forcing the horse to do your bidding, you induce his cooperation by making him your partner and your friend. The way you do that is by speaking his language; gently making sure he understands you and vice versa. This takes time and patience. But eventually, you get a horse who wants to please you. One of the all-time great horse whisperers, and maybe even the original horse whisperer, is a man named Ernesto Rojas, who says, "I teach him what my language is by using his language. . . I become half horse and him half human. That's what I call a union."

Wow, does that sound like the perfect man-woman relationship, or what? It's really just a matter of psychology. But don't get the wrong idea. That doesn't necessarily mean you have to be subtle. Men usually say what they mean and mean what they say, while we females are better at dropping hints and hoping they read between the lines. Chances are you're going to have better luck with your man if you work on being more direct: that is, gently and calmly speaking his language. And, at the same time, you're patterning his behavior with a gentle system of rewards: love, sugar, and a little loosening of the pressure when he does what you want. Followed by a nice massage. Maybe a little beer and sex (for the man, not the horse). In a way, like Ernesto Rojas says, you have to become half woman, half beast.

Here are 10 additional tips:

Be clear and direct when expressing your needs.

Be appreciative when your needs are met.

Be prepared to intuit what his needs are. Just keep your eyes and ears open. He probably is not as knowledgeable about his own needs as you are, or as able to articulate them.

Be sure he knows when he has done the right thing, and when he has done the wrong thing.

Don't over-react.

Be patient. Good partnerships take time.

Never nurse a grudge. Express yourself up front and move on.

Develop a system of rewards that you can both enjoy.

Give as much as you expect to get.

How many times must I say it? Be yourself, know yourself, and in all actions, be true to yourself. Let your Inner Cowgirl guide you.

CHAPTER EIGHTEEN

God and the Cowgirl

*Heaven won't have me and
hell's afraid I'll take over.*
— *Unknown*

The role of God in the Cowgirl's life must not
be underestimated. Do not make the mistake of
thinking that because John Wayne does not go to
church or talk much about God, that God is not
important. For my own part, I believe that part of
being a True Cowgirl is listening to the voice of
God in your own heart, in the wind and the trees,
and in the hearts and voices of others. Sometimes,
when I least expect it, I hear God telling me something. Whether you call it the Great Spirit, the
Great Mother or Father, the Creator, or Whatever,
faith in a Higher Power is the bottom line of a
Cowgirl's life. And for starters, if your man doesn't
feel that way too, no matter how he expresses it in
words, he's probably not the right match for you.

Church itself is a separate, but related, matter.
If nothing else, church will be important after you
have children. For this reason, it was always a
time-tested tenet of my Mama's society-ladies' code
that a woman marry a man not only from the same
religion, but the same denomination. Baptists
marry Baptists, Methodists marry Methodists,
Presbyterians marry Presbyterians. Nowadays, it is
not so critical that you marry exactly your denomination, but it is recommended that you marry a
man with similar religious beliefs.

If he doesn't believe in God and you do, there's
going to be trouble down the road, and I suggest
you stop dating him.

If you have given your life to Jesus and he's

exploring Krishna, I suggest you do not try to save him.

If you are Catholic and he is Jewish, I suggest you have some serious discussions about what that means now, rather than later.

Don't get me wrong – I am not denying that love has the power to conquer all. There are many examples out there of successful mixed-religion couples. I do not judge them and you shouldn't either. But I am here to tell you that married life is hard enough without adding that obstacle to your list of challenges.

I'm here to tell you what the Cowgirl Code is. I didn't make it. It just is. And out on the open range, we believe in God and in the path He has designed for our life.

There are many reasons why church can be important in your dating and married life.

First, there are few places better than church to meet eligible single men. Strange but true. If you ain't tried it, don't knock it.

Second, if you and John Wayne share similar religious beliefs, going to church together can be a powerful growth experience for you as individuals and as a couple.

Third, you're much more likely to get along with his family if you share their beliefs.

Fourth, after you're married, the church provides a healthy social environment you can both indulge in. It provides peer pressure that your cowboy may need to stay on the beam (without you having to play the role of bad cop). And it gives John Wayne some safe buddies to hang around with – the types who will reinforce, rather than tear down, his role in your home and family.

Go to Church and Get Your Reward

★ There are few better venues for meeting decent eligible men.

★ Participating in a church event is a great way to exercise and expand your personal talents.

★ Join him at church for a social activity and you never have to worry about drawing sexual boundaries. They're drawn for you. (And hey, there's no better turn-on than cutting your eyes at each other during service.)

★ You can relax and be yourself when you see him at church because you know you're in a safe environment.

★ You'll probably already know enough about him before the first date so that your chances of success down the road are greater.

★ You may also have an opportunity to meet members of his family in the church setting. If you like them, so much the better. If you spot trouble, you never have to date him at all and will have avoided all that heartache.

★ If you haven't met the Cowboy of Your Dreams at church, take him to church with you. If he's reluctant to go, drop him.

★ If you take John Wayne to church with you and he handles himself well, is polite and makes conversation with a variety of people, this is a good sign. You might want to marry him.

★ If the two of you decide to get married, do it in a church or with a preacher or other spiritual advisor presiding. The vows will be more significant, and the church will give you a solid grounding for your future family – even if your future family consists of a bunch of horses and dogs.

★ After you're married, church provides a solid guardrail to keep you both on the beam. There will be safe friends and good role models for your cowboy, and the same for you. Not to mention your children.

CHAPTER NINETEEN

Tying Your Horse Up (So He Doesn't Wander Away)

Wild oats aren't meant for sowing — but they make a nice trail snack.

— Unknown

Girls, horses are not like dogs. They can't be trained to "Stay." Every woman who rides a horse knows that, no matter how good and loving and obedient your horse, you can't leave him alone and expect him not to wander off. That's just the nature of horses. You gotta tie your horse to something, or at least get someone else to hold the reins if you have to dismount and go do something else for a moment.

The same holds true for your man. Don't get the idea that you can go out every night and party with your friends. Don't get the idea that just because you are shacked up means you are committed. Don't think that just because you are wearing a ring that you can stop your cowboy management program. That would be like buying a horse and then not taking care of it. If you do that, your man will wander away just like any horse, I guarantee it.

Tying Techniques

∩ Make sure you know where he is, no matter how indirectly. Don't let it show that it matters where he is. And don't let it matter, at least in terms of your own security.

∩ Every great once in awhile, when he is at work or at play, show up unexpectedly.

∩ If the two of you are out and some tramp comes on to him, don't brood about it afterward. Show your outrage! Cowboys, just like Cowgirls, like to be reminded they are attractive, and that someone cares enough to be outraged.

∩ If the two of you are out and some ordinary woman talks to him in an ordinary way, don't worry about it. You're big enough to handle it.

∩ If you have complaints about your man, take them to him first; not to your friends or other outsiders.

∩ If you do find that your man has wandered, confront him. Don't be understanding, don't try to find out what you might have "done wrong." Give him an ultimatum. And stick to it. Then make a plan for working out the problems.

∩ It never hurts to flirt with the other cowboys, if you are so inclined.

∩ If you expect him to be true to you, be true to him.

∩ Make sure he knows that you love him.

I have to tell you a story about my friend, Edie, and how she misused sex to manipulate her man, although it all worked out in the end. Edie's live-in boyfriend, Charlie, was a chain-smoker. Edie couldn't stand it. She would open the doors and windows wide even in the cold Wyoming winter, just to get fresh air (and make a point). Finally, she gave Charlie an ultimatum: no sex until you quit smoking. Ordinarily and under general circumstances, I would approve of the giving and withholding of sexual favors as an acceptable way to manipulate your man.

But back to my story. Edie's plan backfired. Charlie went crazy without cigarettes and even crazier without cigarettes and sex. He started to hallucinate, like for real; he saw horns on Edie's head and started chasing her around the house with a broom and calling her Satan (this sounds like fun, but it wasn't). He went on this horrific drunk and didn't come home for several days. Edie was worried sick. She lost so much sleep that she started going crazy, too. Finally Charlie went off for a week. Edie found out through the grapevine that he was shacked up with his best friend's accountant's receptionist, who was also a chain smoker, and they were just lying in bed all day smoking away.

Edie went on the rampage and jumped the bones of the best friend. Charlie heard about that and came home so enraged that, Edie later told me, she thought the two of them were going to end up like the Calico Dog and the Calico Cat, all torn to pieces. What did happen was that instead they tore each other up in bed, just going at each other like sexual maniacs. Edie said she had the imprint of Charlie's cell phone on her back for 24 hours afterward. Well, they got back together after that. Charlie agreed to smoke outside on the porch.

CHAPTER TWENTY

At the End of the Trail, It's All About Grit (and Sugar)

Don't squat with yer spurs on.
— *Unknown*

The oldest Cowgirl I know, Iron-hand Ida, has been married to her husband, Slim, for more than 50 years. They still own a working ranch out near Green River, Wyoming. She's the one who gave me this list of pointers for a lifetime of conjugal bliss. I'm proud to pass them on to you.

Tips for a Happy Lifetime Trail Ride

Never forget Who You Are.

Always be true to Who You Are (your Inner Cowgirl will guide you). Note this does NOT give you permission to be rude, selfish, deceitful, or lazy. A Cowgirl is always polite, generous, honest and hardworking.

Never forget that sex is worthless without romance and trust.

Never underestimate the power of a great home-cooked meal.

Never come between your cowboy and his friends.

Never come between cowboy and his mama.

Do come between cowboy and dangerous other women, doing it by being the best you can be. When necessary, draw your gun.

Never go to bed, hang up the phone, or leave town mad.

- Don't beg or manipulate him into buying you things. Or into doing anything else, for that matter. Trust in, and practice, the power of love.

- Brag about him when you are out with other couples.

- Do NOT brag about him to your single girlfriends.

- Encourage him to pursue hobbies and outside interests. When he announces he has been invited on a fishing trip, be enthusiastic.

- Develop outside interests and hobbies of your own (which you already have, right?).

- Take care of him, and he will take care of you. If he doesn't, tell him what it is you expect him to do.

- Surprise him from time to time.

- Go to church, or in whatever way suits you, pay homage to the Great Spirit.

- Be happy with your home.

- Let him have his own cowboy-spot in your home, and let him keep it however he wants to.

- Don't fight over money. Decide in advance whether you are going to keep your money together or separate. (But even if you decide to keep it together, keep a secret stash for yourself.)

- Try not to let him get fat. But if he does get fat, don't try to make him lose weight. He'll do it when he's ready.

134 • The Cowgirl's Guide to Love

🥾 If he smokes and you don't, let him have a smoking area either in or outside the house.

🥾 If you can afford it, you should each have your own TV.

🥾 If you can afford it, you should each have your own car.

🥾 A kiss in the morning and one at night makes the world all right.

Remember, even after you're married, that you are, and will always be, the most tantalizing girl at the rodeo.

CHAPTER TWENTY-ONE

Calling All Cowgirls

Cowgirl Up!
★

You can share your own experiences, stories, thoughts and philosophies by e-mailing them to: cowgirls@cranehill.com. Check out what your fellow cowgirls are thinking and saying, and get more information about *The Cowgirl's Guide* at our website: www.cranehill.com.

Listed below you will also find the websites used in researching this book. They are another source for expanding your cowgirl horizons — getting to know your fellow cowgirls and learning more about the past, present, and future of cowgirl traditions.

Website Sources

www.adamsmuseumandhouse.org
www.alabamarangers.com
www.angelfire.com
www.babydoe.org
www.bbc.co.uk
www.bbhc.org
www.blackhills-info.com
www.brainyquote.com
www.buffalosoldier.com
www.cattlekate.com

www.cmt.com
www.colorado-mall.com
www.countrystandardtime.com
www.cowboys.com
www.cowgirlchocolates.com
www.cowgirls.com
www.cowgirlsgame.com
www.creativequotations.com
www.dallasnews.com
www.dollyparton.net
www.dorchesterlibrary.org
www.frontiertimes.com
www.frontrangeliving.com
www.genkigirl.com
www.lorettalynn.com
www.nps.gov
www.outlawsandlawmen.com
www.outlawwomen.com
www.patsycline.com
www.readthewest.com
www.ridetheranch.com
www.rockabillyhall.com
www.rootsweb.com
www.royrogers.com
www.salon.com
www.swingin'chicks.com
www.themediadrone.com
www.videoflicks.com

Published Sources

Kirk, Mimi. 2001. *Cowgirl Spirit: Strong Women, Solid Friendship and Stories from the Frontier*. Naperville, Illinois: Sourcebooks.

Montana, Gladiola. 1999. *Grit and Gumption: A Cowgirl's Guide*. Utah: Gibbs Smith.

Savage, Candace. 1996. *Cowgirls*. Berkeley: Ten Speed.

Spinner, Stephanie. 2002. *Who Was Annie Oakley?* New York: Grosset & Dunlap.

Wilson, Ellen. 1962. *Annie Oakley: Young Markswoman*. New York: Aladdin.

About Ellen "Lil" Patrick

Ellen Patrick is the author of more than 20 books of nonfiction and humor for adults and children. Her previous works include *The Southern Rules* (Sweetwater); *The Redneck Night Before Christmas* (Crane Hill); *Help! I'm Southern and I Can't Stop Eating* (Crane Hill); *New Kid in School* (Golden Books); *The Official Digimon Scrapbook* (Scholastic); and *The Very Little Duck* (Simon & Schuster).

Ms. Patrick has lived in every region of the United States, including stints in North Dakota, Vermont, Mississippi, and Utah. She holds a Bachelor's degree in Agricultural Journalism, and has written on farm and ranch topics for the United States Agricultural Extension Service in seven states, and for *Progressive Farmer* magazine. During her youth, she spent a number of summers working as a dude ranch wrangler (where she earned the nickname "Lil") and veterinarian's assistant. She is an avid amateur guitar and harmonica player, storyteller, gospel singer, and gardener.

Lil Patrick lives in New York City, where she is working on a novel and a book of memoirs.